# Polar bears

# Polar bears

by Christina Wilsdon

Reader's
Digest

Published by The Reader's Digest Association, Inc.

London • New York • Sydney • Montreal

# CONTENTS

# A polar bear story

The female polar bear stretched her legs and yawned. She was eager to leave her den in the snow. She had been inside it since October. Now it was March – six months later! Mother Bear could not wait to go outside.

But Mother Bear had not just been napping in the den all winter. She had also given birth to two babies. That was why she had dug the den in the first place.

Mother Bear's two little cubs were born in December. Each one weighed about 0.5kg. They were covered with a thin fuzz instead of fur and could not see or hear. Mother Bear cuddled them close as they drank her rich milk.

Now the babies were busy, furry cubs that could see and hear. Each one weighed almost 14kg – about as much as a human two year old. Like Mother Bear, the cubs were also ready to leave the warm, cosy den.

Mama Bear squirmed through the den's tunnel first. She sniffed the air for danger. Then she moved aside to let Baby Bear and his sister come out.

## Ice bears

The Inuit people of northern Canada call the polar bear *nanuk*, which means 'ice bear'.

At first, Baby Bear was afraid. He pressed close to Mother Bear. So did his sister. The air felt cold and nipped at his ears. Bright light dazzled his eyes.

Mother Bear's stomach rumbled. She had not eaten since October. She had lived off the fat in her body for all these months. But her fat supply was almost all gone now. She was ready to travel to the coast, where she could hunt for seals.

But Baby Bear and his sister could not make this trip yet. They needed more time to get used to being outdoors in the cold. They also needed more time to exercise and strengthen their leg muscles.

So Mother Bear and her babies stayed close to the den for a few weeks. Baby Bear romped and wrestled with his sister. The three bears slept in hollows scraped out of the snow. They went back into the den only when there was a big storm.

## Dig it!

A female polar bear digs her den in a heap of snow. The den usually faces south, towards the sun, to add a bit of extra warmth. The body heat of Mother Bear and her cubs also warms up the den.

## DID YOU KNOW?

**Female polar bears that are going to have babies are the only polar bears that spend the winter in dens. The other polar bears continue to roam and hunt.**

## DID YOU KNOW?

**Polar bears are the biggest bears in the world – bigger even than grizzlies!**

One day, Mother Bear turned to her cubs and made a deep coughing sound. It meant 'Follow me!' Then she set out for the coast. Baby Bear and his sister stepped into the big paw prints she made. Sometimes, when the going was rough, they climbed onto Mother Bear's back, and she carried them through the snow.

Mother Bear had made this trip many times before. She knew that she would find seals along the coast, where they were giving birth to their pups in snow dens on the ice. She would show her cubs how to find these dens and catch the seals inside.

The cubs watched Mother Bear hunt. But they also found lots of time to play.

The two cubs chased each other through the snow. They made holes in the ice by smashing it with their front paws. If they went too far, Mother Bear made a moaning noise to call them back.

When it was time for the cubs to drink some milk, Mother Bear dug a hole in the snow, then sat in it as if it were an armchair. Baby Bear and his sister snuggled close to her.

Baby Bear and his sister will soon start eating meat. They will stop drinking milk but they will not leave Mother Bear. They will stay with her for another two years, learning how to be grown-up polar bears.

## What a meal!

A polar bear can eat as much as 45kg of food at one time.

# The body of a polar bear

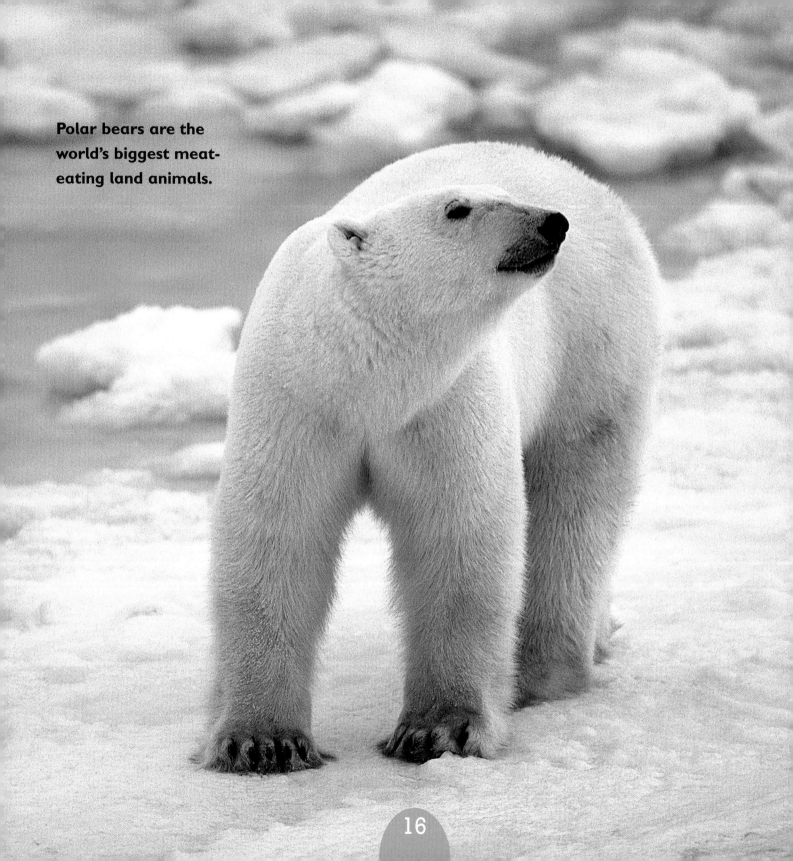

Polar bears are the world's biggest meat-eating land animals.

# Super size

Polar bears live in one of Earth's most severe habitats – the Arctic. The Arctic is a place of ice and snow at Earth's northern tip. In winter, temperatures drop far below freezing. Cold winds and snowstorms sweep the land. Trees cannot grow in the frozen soil. These treeless plains are called tundra.

Polar bears have changed, or adapted, over thousands of years to Arctic life. One adaptation is size. Big bodies lose heat more slowly than small bodies – and polar bears are huge! A male polar bear can weigh from 410kg to 720kg. At 720kg, he would be about half the weight of a medium-sized car!

When standing on all fours, a male polar bear is only about 1.2m high, but he's 3m tall when he stands on his hind legs. A bear this tall would have to duck to go through a doorway without hitting his head! Females are about half the size of males.

## Wedge shape

A polar bear's body is shaped differently than the bodies of other bears. A polar bear's head is longer and more pointed. Its neck is longer, too. This gives the bear a shape like a wedge. Being wedge-shaped helps a polar bear zoom through water when it swims.

# A furry snowsuit

A polar bear is completely covered with fur except for its nose, lips, eyes and the black pads on the bottom of its paws.

The colour of a polar bear's fur helps it to blend in with its environment of snow and ice. The outer fur is made up of long, hollow hairs called guard hairs. Although they look white, guard hairs have no colour – they are clear. Like snow, guard hairs look white because they reflect sunlight. But at sunrise and sunset, a polar bear may look pink or orange – or blue on a foggy day!

Guard hairs also help to waterproof a bear. They are smooth, so water slides off them, preventing it from seeping into the fur and reaching the skin.

Under the guard hairs is a fuzzy layer of fur that helps to hold warm air close to the bear's body. The skin itself is black. This dark skin soaks up heat and light better than pale skin would. The black skin shows through on hairless parts of the bear, such as its nose and lips.

A layer of fat lies under the skin. A well-fed bear may have a fat layer that is 12.5cm thick to help to keep it warm on land and in icy water.

**DID YOU KNOW?**

A polar bear's fur often turns yellow or brown over time as it gets stained by meals of seal fat. Sunlight can also make fur yellow in much the same way that it yellows newspaper.

## Full of fur

This is 1cm². Just one square centimetre of a polar bear's skin can contain about 1,400 hairs!

A polar bear is so warm
inside its 'snowsuit' that it
sometimes rolls in the snow
to cool off!

The fur on the bottom of a polar bear's paws stops the bear from sliding on ice and snow. The black pads are rough with tiny bumps that add extra gripping power.

# Bigfoot bears

A polar bear has gigantic feet. Each paw can be 30cm wide! A polar bear could hide a 30cm ruler just by planting a paw on it.

Big feet are a useful adaptation to life in a land of snow and ice. They work like built-in snowshoes, spreading out the bear's weight so that it does not sink into snow or crash through ice. A polar bear may also shimmy across thin ice on its belly or on its elbows and knees to spread out its weight even more.

Having large paws also helps a polar bear to swim. Its front paws are partly webbed between the toes. The webbing helps the paws to work like flippers when the polar bear dog-paddles in the water. The big back paws are used for steering.

## Paws and claws

Each polar bear paw is tipped with five long, hooked claws. The claws help polar bears to grip the ice. This is especially useful when the polar bear climbs out of the water onto icy ground.

# Polar bears
# on the prowl

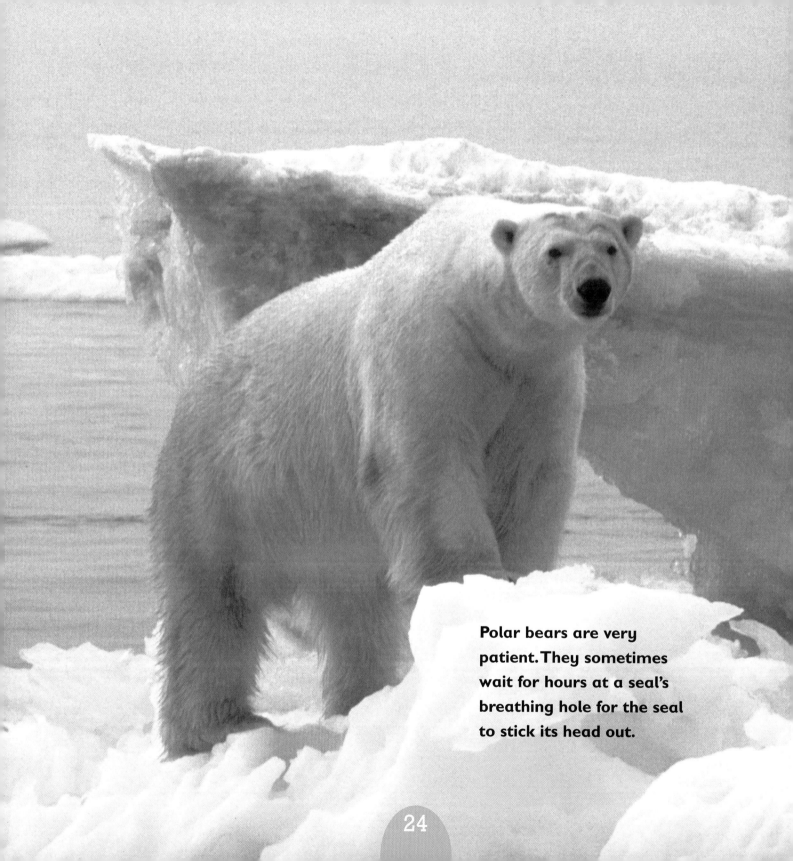

Polar bears are very
patient. They sometimes
wait for hours at a seal's
breathing hole for the seal
to stick its head out.

# Waiting for a meal

The polar bear is a predator – an animal that eats other animals to survive. Its main prey is the ringed seal, but a polar bear will also eat other types of seals.

Ringed seals live throughout the Arctic Ocean. They spend lots of time underwater, but they must come up to breathe. So a ringed seal makes holes in the ice that covers the water. These holes are called breathing holes. A seal pops its head out of a breathing hole to get fresh air. It also enters and exits the water through these holes.

Polar bears know that if they sit and wait by a hole, a seal may pop up. This kind of hunting is called still-hunting.

A polar bear that is still-hunting first finds a hole. It can even sniff out a breathing hole that has been covered by a pile of snow.

Then the bear settles down by the hole to wait. It may sit down or lie on its belly, with its chin resting on the ice. Then it stays perfectly still. It doesn't move a muscle until a seal pokes its head out of the hole. Only then does the bear lunge. It grabs the seal by the head and drags it onto the ice.

# Hunting for a meal

Heaps of snow often drift over breathing holes. In spring, ringed seals carve dens into these drifts and leave their pups to rest inside them. A polar bear that is still-hunting can smell and hear a pup in a den. Quietly, the bear stands up on its hind legs, then smashes open the den with its front paws.

A polar bear also hunts by sneaking up on seals that are lying on the ice. The bear lowers its head, then slowly creeps towards the seal. When very close, the polar bear charges at its prey. Sometimes the seal is able to escape by diving through a breathing hole and disappearing.

A polar bear also sneaks up on resting seals by swimming. The bear paddles quietly up to the edge of the ice. Then it bursts out of the water to grab a seal by surprise.

## Sea bears

Polar bears are very much at home in the sea. In summer, they sometimes spend hours in the water just for fun! They can stay underwater for 2 minutes at a time and swim up to 40 miles without stopping to rest!

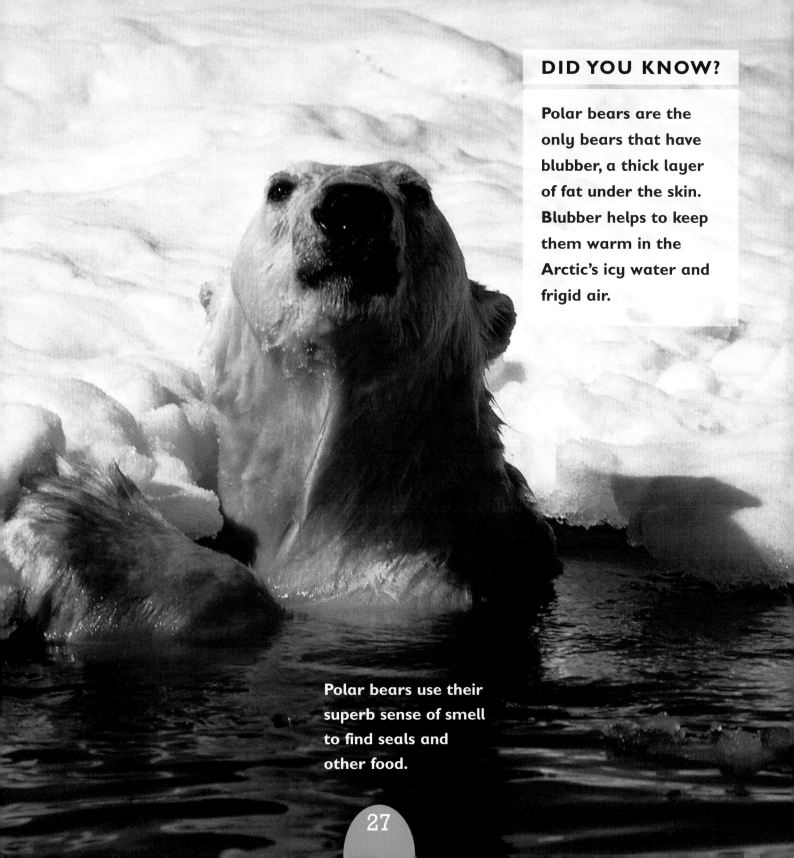

Polar bears are the only bears that have blubber, a thick layer of fat under the skin. Blubber helps to keep them warm in the Arctic's icy water and frigid air.

Polar bears use their superb sense of smell to find seals and other food.

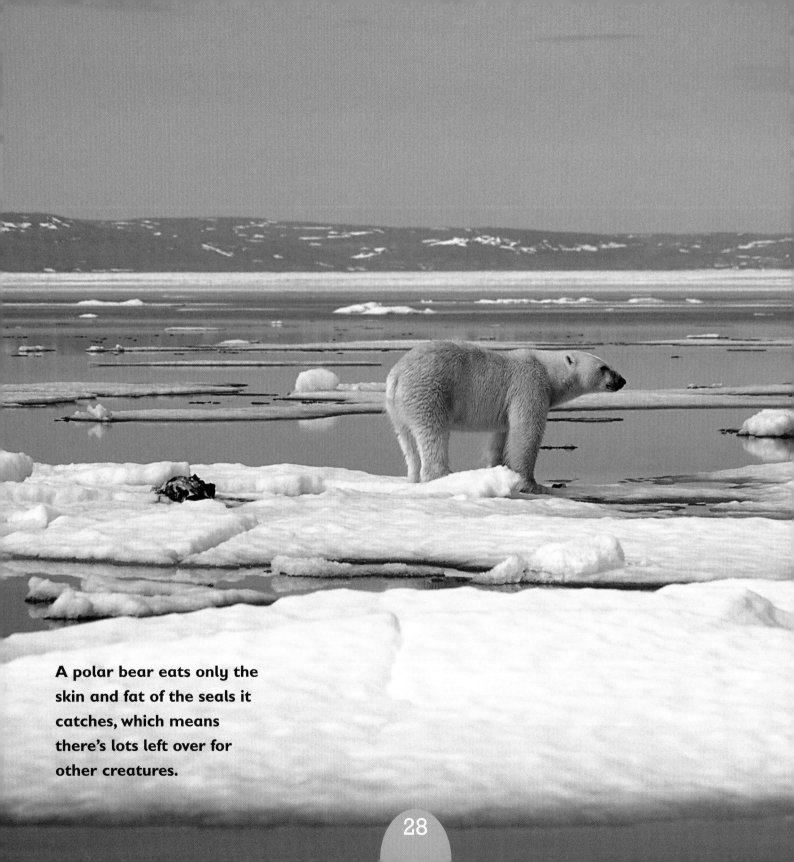

A polar bear eats only the skin and fat of the seals it catches, which means there's lots left over for other creatures.

# Polar bear meals

Polar bears depend on seals for most of their food, but they also eat other animals. Big polar bears prey on adult walruses. Smaller polar bears go after walrus pups. Polar bears sometimes catch white whales called belugas. This happens when belugas get trapped in a small patch of water surrounded by ice. The bears grab the whales and pull them out of the water.

Polar bears also eat fish, seabirds and their eggs, and any leftovers they find. They will travel for miles to feed on a dead whale lying on shore.

A polar bear does not eat every bit of the seals it catches. It usually eats only the seals' fat and skin, not the meat. A polar bear would need much more water than it gets from the seals' fat to digest meat. The polar bear can't drink the seawater because it is salty or eat enough snow to get fresh water because the snow would make the bear too cold.

## Leftover luck

**Arctic foxes closely follow polar bears. They eat any scraps that polar bears leave behind. Gulls and ravens also feed on polar bear meals. Young polar bears eat leftovers from the meals of older bears.**

**Arctic fox**

# Polar bears together

Playtime for male polar bears sometimes means a wrestling match in which they try to knock down the other bear!

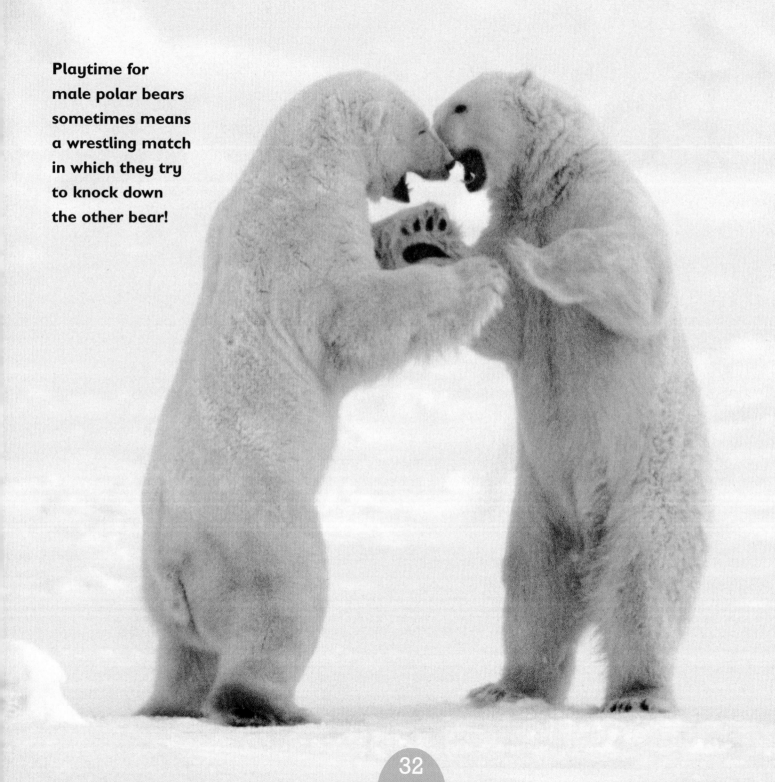

# King of the chill

Polar bears are loners. They do not live in groups. They do not seek out other bears for company. But sometimes even polar bears must spend time with other bears.

Sometimes polar bears see one another when they are hunting for food in the same area. They may seem to form a group if many polar bears come to one place to feed at the same time, but they are not together.

## DID YOU KNOW?

A territory is a place that provides an animal with both a home and food. An animal considers its territory to be its own and will fight to defend it – even against animals of its own kind. Brown bears and black bears each have territories, but polar bears do not. They just head for places where there are lots of seals.

Male polar bears may ignore each other when they meet. But sometimes the two bears play. They stand on their hind legs, shove each other, and try to knock each other down. Scientists have watched bears play for nearly an hour in this way and noticed that the bears do not hurt each other in these fights.

But their play-fighting is also practice for real battles which take place during the mating season, which runs from April to May. Male bears fight fiercely over females during this time. They scratch and bite each other, sometimes leaving scars on their opponent's head and neck. Some males have so many scars from battles in their lives that they look as if they have stripes.

# Bear pairs

A male polar bear uses his sense of smell to find a female bear. He tracks her down, sometimes for miles. A scientist once tracked a male polar bear that walked 60 miles while on the trail of a female bear!

A female bear with cubs will not let a male bear near her. Male bears sometimes hurt or kill cubs. A female will attack a male to drive him away even before he comes close to her family.

However, a female bear without cubs is ready to mate again in spring. Male bears for miles around know this, because as many as six will arrive in her neighbourhood at about the same time. They growl at each other and sometimes fight.

Finally, one male succeeds in chasing away the others. The female polar bear lets the winning male bear come near her. They spend a few days together. Then they part company, each going back to live on its own.

## Grizzly mates

Polar bears and brown bears (grizzlies) sometimes mate. A cub that is half polar bear and half brown bear is often white when it is born. It may grow up to be brownish grey, pale yellow, or even white with brown patches!

A male and female polar bear nuzzle and sniff one another only after the male has chased away any competitors.

Polar bear cubs take naps
just as human children do.

# Care bears

The strongest bond between polar bears is between female bears and their cubs.

Female polar bears are devoted mums. They watch their cubs carefully and warn them away from danger. They chase away male bears that might hurt the cubs. If cubs misbehave, their mother nips them or presses them against the ground.

Cubs spend their first year following close behind their mother. They watch her closely and copy what she does. This is how they learn to hunt. Sometimes cubs get bored sitting quietly. They start playing and spoil their mother's still-hunting!

But cubs learn their hunting lessons well over time. A one-year-old cub can catch a seal pup by itself. A two-year-old cub wanders away from its mother's side and can catch bigger seals.

Most cubs stay with their mothers for two and a half years. They are big enough to take care of themselves by then. Cubs in one part of Canada spend just one and a half years with their mothers. Scientists are studying these bears to find out why.

# Polar bears in the world

# Lands of ice and snow

Polar bears live where it is cold most of the year and the ocean is covered with large sheets of ice, called floes. In autumn, polar bears move from land to floes that form near shores. They look for seals in big cracks in the floes and for seals' breathing holes.

In spring, sea ice melts in southern parts of the polar bears' world. The bears travel farther north to find ice that is still solid.

In some places, all the sea ice melts, and polar bears must stay on land until the water freezes again.

# Where polar bears live

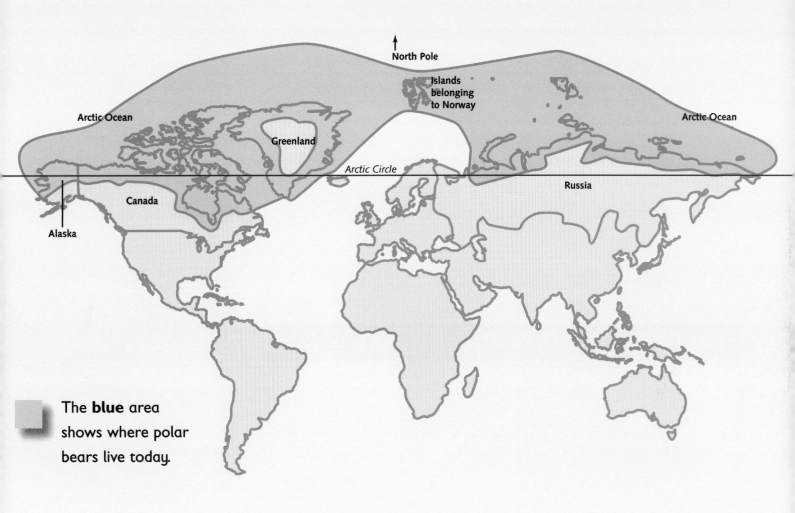

North Pole

Islands belonging to Norway

Arctic Ocean

Greenland

Arctic Ocean

Arctic Circle

Russia

Canada

Alaska

The **blue** area shows where polar bears live today.

Polar bears live mainly in the Arctic. The Arctic lies above a line marked on maps that is called the Arctic Circle. Trees do not grow above this line.

Polar bears live along Arctic coastlines in Canada, Russia, Greenland and islands belonging to Norway. They also live in Alaska.

# Polar bears – the future

Nations with polar bears signed The International Agreement on the Conservation of Polar Bears in 1973 to control hunting and to protect polar bear habitat. But the biggest threat is still damage to their habitat caused by oil spills, pollution and global warming.

In Canada, ice is melting sooner in spring and later in autumn so the bears' vital seal-hunting season is now shorter. Shrinking ice elsewhere in the Arctic means they have to swim farther to reach ice and may drown. Their future hinges on finding ways to slow climate change.

## FAST FACTS ABOUT POLAR BEARS

| | |
|---|---|
| **SCIENTIFIC NAME** | *Ursus maritimus* |
| **CLASS** | Mammals |
| **ORDER** | Carnivora |
| **SIZE** | Females up to 2.5m long |
| **WEIGHT** | Males to 720kg<br>Females to 400kg |
| **LIFE SPAN** | 15-18 years in the wild<br>30 years in captivity |
| **HABITAT** | Arctic tundra and pack ice |
| **TOP SPEED** | 25 miles per hour |

## Stop global warming, save the polar bear

Many people are working to find ways to slow global warming and hope polar bears will benefit from their work. In small ways, you can help too:

- Put on a sweater instead of turning up the heat.
- Turn off your TV and computer when not using them.
- Recycle cans, bottles, paper and other items.
- Take a quick shower instead of a bath.

## DID YOU KNOW?

● Because polar bears spend so much time in ocean waters, scientists call them marine mammals. The word marine means 'about the sea'.

● The polar bear's scientific name, *Ursus maritimus*, means 'sea bear' in Latin.

# GLOSSARY OF WILD WORDS

| | |
|---|---|
| adaptation | a change over time in an animal's body or behaviour that helps it to survive in its habitat |
| arctic | northern lands and oceans where it is cold and snowy much of the year |
| blubber | a thick layer of fat under the skin that helps to keep an animal warm |
| boar | a male bear |

| | |
|---|---|
| breathing hole | a hole that a seal digs in the ice to use as an entrance and exit as well as for coming up for air |
| conservation | the protection and preservation of land, animals, plants and other natural resources |
| cub | a baby bear |
| floes | sheets of ice on the ocean |
| global warming | an increase in the average temperature of the Earth that causes a change in climate |

| | | | |
|---|---|---|---|
| guard hairs | long hairs that form the outer layer of a polar bear's fur | species | a group of living things that are the same in many ways |
| habitat | the natural environment where an animal or plant lives | still-hunting | a way of hunting that involves sitting still and waiting by a seal's breathing hole |
| Inuit | native people (Eskimos) of northern Canada, Alaska and parts of Greenland | tundra | a big area of land in the Arctic region with no trees and a permanently frozen layer of soil |
| predator | an animal that hunts and eats other animals to survive | wedge | something that is thicker at one end and thinner at the other |
| prey | animals that are eaten by other animals | | |

# INDEX

**Polar Bears** is an ***All About Animals*** fact book
Written by Christina Wilsdon

Published in 2010 in the United Kingdom by Vivat Direct Limited (t/a Reader's Digest),
157 Edgware Road, London W2 2HR

Editor: Rachel Warren Chadd
Designer: Nicola Liddiard
Art editor: Simon Webb

Printed and bound in Europe by Arvato Iberia

ISBN: 978 0 276 44616 0
Book code: 640-025 UP0000-1
Oracle code: 504500025H.00.24